NORTH AMERICA'S LOST DECADE?

NORTH AMERICA'S LOST DECADE?

PAUL KRUGMAN AND DAVID ROSENBERG VS. LAWRENCE SUMMERS AND IAN BREMMER

THE MUNK DEBATE ON THE NORTH AMERICAN ECONOMY

EDITED BY RUDYARD GRIFFITHS AND PATRICK LUCIANI

ANANSI

This edition published in 2012 by
House of Anansi Press Inc.
110 Spadina Avenue, Suite 801
Toronto, ON, M5V 2K4
Tel. 416-363-4343
Fax 416-363-1017
www.houseofanansi.com

Distributed in Canada by
HarperCollins Canada Ltd.
1995 Markham Road
Scarborough, ON, M1B 5M8
Toll free tel. 1-800-387-0117

Distributed in the United States by
Publishers Group West
1700 Fourth Street
Berkeley, CA 94710
Toll free tel. 1-800-788-3123

House of Anansi Press is committed to protecting our natural environment.
As part of our efforts, this book is printed on paper that contains 100%
post-consumer recycled fibres, is acid-free, and is processed chlorine-free.

16 15 14 13 12   1 2 3 4 5

Library and Archives Canada Cataloguing in Publication

North America's lost decade? : the Munk debate on the North American economy /
Rudyard Griffiths and Patrick Luciani, editors.

(The Munk debates)
Based on the "Be it resolved North America faces a Japan-style
era of high unemployment and slow growth", Munk Debate
held on Nov. 14, 2011.
Issued also in electronic format.

ISBN 978-1-77089-200-2

1. North America — Economic conditions. 2. United States — Economic
conditions — 2009-. 3. United States — Economic conditions — 2001–2009.
I. Griffiths, Rudyard II. Luciani, Patrick III. Series: Munk debates

HC95.N659 2011   330.97'00541   C2011-907741-8

Library of Congress Control Number: 2011943046

Cover design: Alysia Shewchuk
Text design: Colleen Wormald
Typesetting: Alysia Shewchuk
Transcription: Rondi Adamson

 Canada Council
for the Arts
Conseil des Arts
du Canada

 ONTARIO ARTS COUNCIL
CONSEIL DES ARTS DE L'ONTARIO

*We acknowledge for their financial support of our publishing program
the Canada Council for the Arts, the Ontario Arts Council,
and the Government of Canada through the Canada Book Fund.*

Printed and bound in Canada

 MIX
Paper from
responsible sources
FSC
www.fsc.org FSC® C004071

 ANCIENT FOREST ™
FRIENDLY

CONTENTS

INTRODUCTION BY PETER MUNK

The United States and the world are still suffering the consequences of the financial crises that started in late 2008. With slow economic recovery, high unemployment, collapsing equity and real estate prices, a growing national debt, and a politically divided Congress, the United States is struggling to find the right policies to get its economy back on track. And even though Canada has managed to avoid the worst of the financial crisis, if the United States doesn't get it right, we will all be in for a difficult time.

That was the background to the eighth semi-annual Munk Debate held at Roy Thomson Hall in Toronto on November 14, 2011, before an audience of 2,700 with many thousands more following online. The resolution that night was "Be it resolved North America faces a Japan-style era of high unemployment and slow growth." Is the same fate awaiting the United States as it grapples with a similar crisis that threatens to bring down its economy? Or will America's creativity, ingenuity, and free markets rally to find solutions to overcome the worst financial and economic crisis since the Great Depression?

America's challenge is made more difficult as the European experiment, with its common currency, comes under tremendous stress as member countries struggle to get their debt levels under control. And whatever one thinks of the "Occupy Movement" and its bizarre mixture of social, political, and economic messages, it has one complaint in common with the Tea Party movement: something has to be done to restrain the risk-taking and excesses of the financial sector so that it doesn't bring the "real" economy down with it. As with Japan, both the eurozone and the United States have accumulated massive public debt as a result of bailouts and fiscal stimuli while revenues have declined. What makes matters more concerning is that the United States has never had a recovery without the help of a surge in the real estate market, but a strong recovery in housing doesn't seem likely any time soon.

Four exceptional thinkers were selected to debate these crucial issues. Arguing for the resolution was Nobel laureate Paul Krugman and economist and investment strategist David Rosenberg.

Anyone who keeps up with the American political scene and economy knows the work of Paul Krugman. Not only does he write a highly influential *New York Times* column, but he is also Professor of Economics at

Princeton University. For his scholarship he was awarded the Nobel Prize in Economics in 2008. Dr. Krugman is a bestselling author of a number of acclaimed books and an acknowledged expert and observer of the Japanese economy. Paul Krugman reminds us that the situation in the United States is far worse than that of Japan in the early 1990s, and he doesn't see a solution as long as there is a deadlock between the Republicans and Democrats on economic policy. He also makes the argument that following a financial crisis — at least since WWII — countries have only recovered by running large trade surpluses, an option not open to the United States.

Debating with Dr. Krugman is Canadian David Rosenberg, Chief Economist and Strategist of the Toronto-based wealth management firm Gluskin Sheff and Associates. David also served as Chief North American Economist at Bank of America Merrill Lynch. An exceptional analyst, he is one of only a handful of economists who predicted the slow pace of the post-crisis recovery and the stark reversal in stock valuations. Mr. Rosenberg is right to remind us that massive fiscal stimulus in the United States won't be effective in getting the economy to grow in the face of a massive consumer de-leveraging of private debt.

Arguing against the resolution were Lawrence Summers and Ian Bremmer who believe that North America's economy and institutions are flexible enough to weather the current storm. Lawrence Summers came to this debate with a sterling reputation as an economic scholar and public servant, and I am personally gratified that he accepted our invitation to participate. He is also a respected economic theorist who served as President of Harvard University, Chief Economist at the World Bank, and as Secretary of the Treasury of the United States under President Bill Clinton. More recently, he served as director of President Obama's National Economic Council.

Dr. Summers holds the opposing view that the housing collapse and the drop in the stock market in Japan during the 1990s were much deeper than they are in the United States today. He doesn't view the political crisis in the United States as pessimistically as the pro side, he believes that America is still the place where everyone with ambition, creativity, and hope wants to come to live and invest, despite its economic problems.

Ian Bremmer's intelligence, insight, and wisdom as a political analyst belie his age. He is a bestselling author and an insightful commentator on politics and the economy in the United States, and over the last decade, he has started and turned his Eurasia Group into a leading global risk research and consulting firm. Mr. Bremmer admits that the United States is facing deficit and unemployment issues, but he argues that when the world gets nervous they always turn to the US dollar as a safe haven, a huge economic benefit not available to Japan.

Who's right? How will things turn out? Although I am confident that American institutions will prevail through hard work and innovation, it will take exceptional leadership south of the border. As Churchill once said, "You can always count on Americans to do the right thing — after they've tried everything else."

We don't know if the U.S. economy can be put on track to lower unemployment while controlling the growth of the national debt, but we are certain these transcripts highlight the extraordinary challenges facing the North American economy. The debate in these pages leads to a better understanding of the solutions that might help us avoid the fate of the Japanese economy.

As I have said a number of times, when we started holding these debates our intention was a simple one: to bring the finest thinkers debating the crucial questions facing our world. In that respect, we have exceeded our expectations in the span of a few short years. And for that I have to credit my Aurea Foundation's Board, more specifically, Rudyard Griffiths who has done a wonderful job of moderating these events. I am proud of our Foundation's debate series, and, as ever, I am grateful to our speakers for an exceptional evening of discussion, excitement, and — yes — entertainment.

Peter Munk
Founder, the Aurea Foundation
Toronto, December 2011

North America's Lost Decade?

Pro: Paul Krugman and David Rosenberg
Con: Lawrence Summers and Ian Bremmer

November 14, 2011
Toronto, Canada

THE MUNK DEBATE ON THE NORTH AMERICAN
ECONOMY

RUDYARD GRIFFITHS: Ladies and gentlemen, welcome to Roy Thomson Hall in Toronto, Canada, for the Munk Debate on the North American economy. My name is Rudyard Griffiths, and I'm the co-organizer of this debate series along with my colleague, Patrick Luciani. It is my privilege to be your moderator once again.

I want to start by welcoming the more than 4,000 people who have logged on to the Internet to watch this debate live on BNN.ca and on theglobeandmail.com. Hello also to the North America-wide audience that is tuning in to watch or listen to this debate in Canada on the Business News Network (BNN), CBC Radio's *Ideas* program, or on CPAC (the Cable Public Affairs Channel), and throughout the continental United States on C-SPAN.

Finally, I'd like to say hello to the 2,700 people that have filled Roy Thomson Hall to capacity, for the third time in a row, for a Munk Debate. Those of us responsible for organizing the series would like to claim credit for coming up with the topic and selecting the presenters that sold out this hall in a little less than seventy-two hours, but don't worry, we know better. Let's face it: everybody is here for one simple reason, one simple fact. We're worried. We're worried about the impact of the European debt crisis on our own economic recovery; we're concerned about the slow pace of recovery, the slow pace of job creation and economic growth, a full three years after the financial crisis.

I'll bet some of you in the audience are starting to worry at a more fundamental level that the prosperity that we've enjoyed in North America — incredible prosperity for going on five decades — has come to an end. Are this continent's best days behind it instead of ahead of it?

As vexing as these economic concerns are, they need to be set against one simple fact: we are North Americans. We live and work in one of the most open, prosperous, and technologically advanced regions in the world. We live in a society that enjoys a resilient workforce, and has an incredible capacity for innovation. As a result, we have an economy that is envied by developed and developing nations alike.

Ladies and gentlemen, this is the crux of tonight's debate for your organizers. Can the long-standing and considerable strengths of our economy adapt to the new challenges it faces both internally and internationally, thereby powering a new era of growth and prosperity?

4

Or are the economic anxieties that we feel today somehow predictive of the future, thereby making the motion "Be it resolved North America faces a Japan-style era of high unemployment and slow growth" an accurate forecast of our common economic future?

In a moment I'm going to introduce the roster of world-class presenters that we've assembled to weigh in on this all-important debate. But first let me recognize the two people who alone are responsible for staging these debates. It is thanks to their generosity and their public-spiritedness that we are able to bring some of the brightest thinkers and sharpest minds to Toronto to weigh in on the big questions and problems facing Canada and the world. So please join me in a round of appreciation and applause for our hosts, Peter and Melanie Munk.

Tonight, arguing for the motion are Nobel laureate Paul Krugman and David Rosenberg. Arguing against the motion, Ian Bremmer and Lawrence Summers.

Let me briefly introduce our debaters. Paul Krugman is the 2008 Nobel laureate for Economic Sciences. His highly influential *New York Times* column is a must-read for anyone interested in U.S. politics and economics. In addition to his massive body of scholarly work — he has published twenty scholarly books and two hundred academic papers — he is the author of numerous bestsellers, including *The Return of Depression Economics and the Crisis of 2008*. Equally important to us, Dr. Krugman has a long-standing interest and policy engagement with the causes and consequences of Japan's lost decade.

Canadian David Rosenberg is the chief economist and strategist of the Toronto-based wealth management firm Gluskin Sheff and Associates. Before joining Gluskin Sheff, David was the chief North American economist at Bank of North America. Let me mention that David is one of only a handful of economists to predict both the anemic pace of the post-crisis recovery and the economic reversal in stock valuations.

Let me introduce the debaters arguing against the motion. Ian Bremmer is an acclaimed author and the founder and head of the Eurasia Group, the world's leading global risk research and consulting firm. Two of his internationally bestselling books are especially relevant to this debate: *The J Curve: A New Way to Understand Why Nations Rise and Fall* and *The End of the Free Market: Who Wins the War between States and Corporations?* Ian writes a regular column on geopolitics for the *Financial Times* of London and the influential *The Call* blog for *Foreign Policy*.

Our final debater tonight, Lawrence Summers, was hailed by the *Globe and Mail* as being to the economics profession what previous Munk debater Henry Kissinger is to the practice of international diplomacy. He is one of North America's most respected economists, having published widely in the areas of public finance and macroeconomics. His public service career spans a variety of posts, including chief economist at the World Bank, U.S. Treasury secretary under president Bill Clinton, president of Harvard, and most recently as the head of President Obama's influential National Economic Council.

Now, let me briefly run down how the debate is going to unfold. Each debater has six minutes for opening statements to make their case for and against the motion. After opening statements, we're going to have our debaters challenge each other's key arguments and tackle pointed questions from some notable audience members. Our debate will conclude with short closing statements from each debater — this time only three minutes each — and a second audience vote on the motion.

Speaking of votes, let's find out how this audience of 2,700 voted on the motion going into this debate. The audience voted 55 percent in favour of the motion — they are a somewhat pessimistic group; 25 percent voted against, and 20 percent were undecided. On the second question, 95 percent of the audience were open to changing their minds. In other words, this audience is open minded.

Ladies and gentlemen, we officially have a debate on our hands. We agreed in advance on the order of speakers, so, Mr. Krugman, I'm going to start with you.

PAUL KRUGMAN: I hope you'll let me start with a judgement. If the audience says they are open minded, at least 50 percent of them are lying. Also, I've been asked if this debate is about North America, but it's going to be about the United States. I apologize for that. Canada doesn't really fit in for two reasons. One, it's small, and two, it has not messed up enough to be interesting, so this is going to be a U.S.-centred discussion.

Let me say I find it quite strange, at this point, that people are still wondering whether things can go as badly in the United States as they have in Japan, because the fact is that things in the United States have already gotten much, much worse than they ever did in Japan. It's startling to look back on Japan's troubles, and they were real, but Japan never had the kind of drastic slump in employment that has afflicted the United States. It never had a decline in real GDP, comparable to what the United States is experiencing, until the world went into crisis in 2008.

So the United States has had a bad start already, much worse than anything Japan has had. Will the United States recover quickly from this shock? It's too late for that. It's already been four years since the great recession began. Are we feeling prosperous yet? There's not even a hint that a V-shaped recovery is taking place in the United States right now. The kind of thing that we hoped would happen isn't even in the offing or on the horizon. For the past two and a half years the United States has basically been in a holding pattern; growing, but not fast enough to make any significant dent in unemployment, which remains very high.

It's not a collapsing economy, but a sour economy. That's what a lost decade looks like. That's what Japan looked like during this period, except that the United States is sourer and more lost than Japan ever was. Why would we think that things would get any better? Some analysts say that in the United States assets have never fallen as much and our stock market has never plunged

8

as low as that of the Japanese. Let me offer a couple of answers on these points. One is that Japan took a long time to get as bad as it is right now. If you go back to the 1990s, the Nikkei Index was above 15,000 for almost all of that decade.

You can say that America was a lot more vulnerable to a falling asset crisis because our households never saved much in the first place. But ultimately you have to judge these things on a PPE basis. That's "proof of the pudding is in the eating," and evidence suggests that the United States had a bigger shock to its economy than Japan did when its bubble burst. Another point is that for the first fifteen years of its lost decade — Japan's lost decade is now in its nineteenth year — Japan had a great advantage: its economic woes were unique, so it could, to some extent, pull itself out by exporting to countries that were more prosperous.

As far as I can tell, the countries involved in every financial crisis since World War II have recovered by having an export boom, by having a large trade surplus compared to the rest of the world. This time around there is no one to whom we can sell. We're all involved in this crisis, so the United States can't pull itself out by running a trade surplus unless we can find another planet to sell to.

So, what is it about the American situation that would make us think that we're going to do any better and that North America is not going to have a lost decade? There is the claim that America is a more dynamic and creative society than Japan, which is arguably true, but that

9

was also true of America in the 1930s. We were very dynamic and very creative then, and it still took a war to end the Depression. Mainly, though, what I hear is the claim that American policy has been, or will be, better than Japanese policy. My answer to that is *say what?*

Yes, the Fed, my former department head, Ben Bernanke, [chairman of the Federal Reserve] was quicker on the draw than his predecessors and his counterparts at the Bank of Japan — he dropped interest rates to zero quickly, and obviously that wasn't enough. That happened three years ago. Arguably, America's done a better job at not perpetuating zombie banks, but if you were to do a serious analysis of Japan, you would know that the issue was greatly overrated in the first place.

Where fiscal policy is concerned — which can be most effective — we criticize Japan for having a "stop-go" approach in their stimulus programs that were inadequate, and then pulling them back before the economy was truly on the road to recovery. We've done the same thing — U.S. fiscal policy has turned strongly contrarian at this point, with the Obama stimulus plan fading out and state and local governments continuing to contract.

So if you want to believe that America is going to do better, you have to believe that we are going to reach a consensus on stronger, more effective policy. You have to believe that the American political system is heading towards that kind of effective consensus. And I guess the question is, looking at American politics, what would make you think that it's headed towards a consensus for effective action? What would even make you think it's headed towards sanity? In recent polls, Newt Gingrich [former Speaker of the U.S. House of Representatives] has pulled into the lead for the Republican nomination. So I see absolutely no reason to believe that America will do better than Japan.

RUDYARD GRIFFITHS: Larry Summers, you are next.

LAWRENCE SUMMERS: Paul, I would buy, not sell. You're right — the United States has a serious demand deficiency. You're right that not enough is being done to contain this demand deficiency. You're right that we will suffer needless unemployment and stagnation until more is done to address demand deficiency. You're right in what you have written, and there is an analogy that you and I have shared, quoting Keynes.[1]

Keynes famously described Britain's problems as a "magneto" problem. That was British-speak, circa 1931, for a problem with the electrical system of a car. His point was that if your car wouldn't go and you fixed the electrical system, then it would, and you didn't have to engage in a fundamental and far-reaching critique of your car. You only had to fix what was wrong. When an economy like that of the United States suffers from low aggregate demand, you only have to fix what is wrong and move to strengthen demand.

---

[1] British economist John Maynard Keynes (1883–1946). His advocacy of governmental monetary and fiscal programs to stimulate employment and spending dominated Western economic policy from the immediate postwar years to the early 1970s.

My thesis is that as serious as the demand problem is, it is dimensionally much less than the problems that Japan faced in four respects. Japan's problems were different in magnitude, different in the depth of their structural roots, different in the relative perspective they had — relative to the rest of the world — and different in the degree of resilience their system had for adapting.

Let's get the magnitude straight. In Japan, house prices fell to a level not two-thirds of previous levels but to 15 percent of previous levels. The U.S. stock market may get there, but to get where it got in Japan you have to be talking about Dow 2,600, and I don't think that is in the cards. Paul, in 1994, you forecasted — and your forecasts were very close to the kinds of estimates the Clinton administration made — that Japanese potential GDP growth would be 3 percent or a bit more. By that standard, Japan is now producing half of the potential output that people were forecasting when its lost decade began. That's a problem of a different magnitude than the U.S. gap, serious though it is, at 6 or 7 percent.

There is little wonder that Japan's slowdown is so profound, given the magnitude of the structural problems that hold Japan back. It is the most rapidly ageing society in the industrialized world, resulting in slow labour-force growth; Japan has epic insularity and an inability to accept immigration; there has been a massive retrenchment by its companies to their home markets, and an utter lack of capacity for entrepreneurial innovation in the era of the social network. The United States still remains the only country in the world where you can raise your first hundred million dollars before you buy your first suit and tie.

Let's look at relative perspective. When Japan's economy went wrong in the 1990s, the world was working. The United States was flourishing and growing. Europe was flourishing and growing. It was Japan that was having a substantial reduction in its share of the GDP of the industrialized world. It's very different now. The United States' problems are the problems of every industrial democracy. And the U.S. share of the industrial world is steadily increasing.

There's plenty that is wrong with the U.S. political system, but if you consider that there were eight prime ministers in as many years in Japan, and consider what has passed for governance in Europe in recent years, I would suggest that our problems do not loom large relative to either the economics or to the politics in the rest of the world. We remain completely unlike Japan. North America remains the place where everyone in the world wants to come, and the place where everyone in the world wants to put their money.

Finally, we are a uniquely resilient society, and we have seen this before. President John F. Kennedy died believing that Russia would surpass the United States by the early 1980s. Every issue of the *Harvard Business Review* published in 1991 proclaimed that the Cold War was over and that Japan and Germany had won, and that was before the best decade in U.S. economic history.

It will take time. There are steps that need to be taken, but we are a society that works. We are a society whose principal problems — everyone on stage with me agrees — can be addressed by a change in the printing of money and the creation of infrastructure. That is not the kind of fundamental problem Japan has.

RUDYARD GRIFFITHS: Next is David Rosenberg.

DAVID ROSENBERG: Thank you. My colleague and partner Paul Krugman said that the "proof of the pudding was in the eating," and that certainly resonates because the proof is this: we have had three years of unprecedented and radical stimulus in the economy. We've had policy rates in the United States at zero percent for three years. Who predicted those rates four, five, six, seven years ago? The Federal Reserve has taken its balance sheet into the stratosphere. What was once an 800-billion-dollar stable balance sheet is now sitting at two and a half trillion dollars. We've had, at the same time, three years of government deficits in the United States at the federal level of more than 10 percent of GDP. President Roosevelt never ran the deficit above 6 percent for one year in the New Deal.

We've had three years of unprecedented fiscal stimulus, yet what did we get out of it? What did we squeeze out of the lemon? What we got was real GDP growth of barely more than 2 percent at an average annual rate. Take a look at what is normal historically. What is normal in the context of a post–World War II, post-recession recovery, nine quarters in, as we are today? Normal is 5.5 percent.

We've averaged barely more than 2 percent despite the most radical government incursion into the economy that we've ever seen. If this were a garden-variety business cycle, with that degree of stimulus, we'd actually have GDP growth running at an annual rate of 8.5 percent, and we'd be talking about hyperinflation. This is what makes this experience similar, though it's not exactly the same as the Japanese experience. No two cycles are exactly the same.

What this tells us, despite all these policy tailwinds and the lack of potential GDP growth that has left the unemployment rate around 9 percent for thirty months now, is that our policy-makers are bumping against the severe headwinds otherwise known as the debt de-leveraging cycle. We still have a depression in housing four years after the initial detonation. And we have unprecedented proportions of consumer debt de-leveraging in the United States. We had a forty-year secular credit expansion that went absolutely parabolic in 2002, because we had a government that believed that as an antidote to burst the dot.com bubble we could save the system by engineering a financial and housing bubble.

The basic problem that we have on our hands is that the largest component of the U.S. economy, called the U.S. household sector — it is 70 percent of GDP — is trying desperately to get out of debt. How do you get out of debt? Well, you either pay it down, which comes at the expense of other spending, or you default.

What does a credit de-leveraging cycle mean? (By the way, we have not had this situation at any other time in the post–World War II period. You have to go back almost to the previous century.) It means the paying down of debt. It means rising savings rates. It means reorienting the family budget away from luxury goods and services towards necessities. It means a weak economic backdrop, and it is fundamentally deflationary.

Japan went through an asset bubble that burst. I'm not going to try and get into the parameters of what was bigger and what was smaller. But Japan went through a massive credit de-leveraging that is ongoing. That's exactly what is happening in the United States, and that's what has held back the economy despite the stimulus. So far the household sector has paid down or walked away from de-leveraging roughly one trillion dollars.

If we're talking about the concept of mean reversion — and mean reversion is very important in this business — then we're talking about taking debt to asset and debt to income ratios back to their pre-bubble norms. I believe this is going to happen, but there will be at least another three trillion dollars of de-leveraging. The question is going to be whether the fiscal policy outlook and the monetary policy outlook are going to survive long enough to act as antidotes to this de-leveraging cycle.

How long do de-leveraging cycles last? Well, I have this old saying: "when in doubt, rely on somebody else's work." The Mackenzie Group did this work two years ago, and they found that you can have the assumption of a plain, vanilla, garden-variety business cycle — in which case we'd be off to the races by now, but we are not — or you can have a credit and asset shock. Home prices went down 35 percent this cycle, more than they did in the 1930s. Working through these asset and credit cycles takes roughly seven years, so we have finished two cycles already. I'm going to be optimistic and say only five more to go.

RUDYARD GRIFFITHS: Ian Bremmer of the Eurasia Group, you are up next for the final opening statement.

IAN BREMMER: Last I read, the proposition was on North America. Some of us think it's the fifty-first state up here, but I do want to mention Canada. I'll save it for the end: best for last.

As Rudyard said, we're very concerned about the economy. I understand why there's negativity. We're concerned about the world. The architecture that was created after World War II by the United States isn't working the way it used to. We call it the World Bank to sound global; we call it the World Series too. Even though there is a Canadian team in professional baseball, we know the truth.

There is creative destruction happening in the global environment today and we don't like that. If Americans had a choice to go back to when all that architecture was functioning well — ten years ago, twenty years ago, thirty years ago — that would be a more comfortable world. But that is not what we are debating. What we are debating is whether or not we can feel good about the world now.

Where are we going to invest, where are we going to live? Where do we want to give our kids a chance to make their mark? That's a relative game, and Larry and I bet firmly on North America and we bet firmly on the United States. Why do we do that? Where else are you going? I look at Europe, and there are seventeen nations in the eurozone and they talk about fiscal unity. Fiscal unity is not the problem in Europe. The problem in Europe is that there is no kids' table. There are seventeen countries and there is no kids' table. When I was a kid they did not give me sharp utensils because the family pet would have been hurt. In Europe there's Greece and Italy. There are seventeen countries and they all have breakable glassware — that doesn't make sense. That is going to take years to sort out.

Paul Krugman recently said, "It's ending not with a bang but with bunga, bunga." I read that piece and I thought, wow, he wouldn't go to Europe. How about Japan? Seventeen prime ministers in twenty-two years. That is a modern-day Asian record if you don't include military coups in Thailand, which I am not wont to do.

For fifty years they had a single-party system, the Liberal Democratic Party (LDP). Suddenly it's gone. But they don't have public policy schools. The Democratic Party of Japan doesn't know how to govern. That's why they're going through so many prime ministers right now. They don't have connections with the bureaucrats that actually understand policy, nor do they have connections with Japanese industrialists. So you're not betting on Japan.

How about China? You did that debate already. I saw it and I know how you voted. You're not betting on a Chinese century and you're not betting on a Chinese era. You're not betting on it because China is massively volatile. They've got to move from a state capitalist system to a consumption-based system. They have to change not only their economic system, but they have to adapt their political system. Maybe they can do it, but with 1.3 billion people? This has never been done before. I'd put 5 percent of my portfolio on it. I wouldn't invest the nest egg. That would be crazy.

Now, the United States has problems. Larry and I are not saying that the United States doesn't have problems. There are deficit issues, unemployment issues, and governance issues. We're not happy with where Congress is right now, but there's a difference between that and fearmongering. Look at the United States, and, in terms of governance, we all went crazy, "Oh, the debt limit! It's going to explode!" Then, of course, at the last minute, they pull out a deal. We're saying the same thing right now. Nine days down the road we're going to have a super committee; it's going to explode. We'll get our 1.2 trillion. It's going to be ugly. It's not a great way to govern. But it's better than what we see in Japan, Europe, or China.

There's an easy way to look at this. It's called the dollar. Where do people go during this time of concern? They go to the dollar or they go to gold. And you know what? The last time I checked, gold isn't a country.

I said I wanted to spend a little time on Canada. I

got the *Globe and Mail* delivered to my hotel room this morning, and on the front page it said that the prime minister stands by President Obama but looks to Asia. Canada can hedge. Canada's got the United States but as of May 2011, it has also got British Columbia selling more timber to China than to the United States.

Energy goes everywhere. You don't do Keystone right now, but you build on infrastructure. Last time I was in Calgary the Chinese were doing everything possible to get in and buy, buy, buy. Does anybody really believe Canada is entering a lost era? I don't buy it.

RUDYARD GRIFFITHS: Ian, thank you — a strong finish to our opening statements, and I think we can sense the tension between the two sides. So what we're going to do now is take a few questions, get these debaters jousting with each other. To get us going, I want to have both teams react to a quote about the threat the eurozone crisis presents to global economic recovery. The quote is, "The economy around the world runs the risk of a downward spiral of uncertainty, financial instability, and potential collapse of global demand. We run the risk of what some are calling the 'lost decade.'" These words were spoken last week by none other than Christine Lagarde, the head of the International Monetary Fund (IMF).

Larry, let me ask: why is Lagarde wrong to invoke the spectre of a lost decade when it comes to interpreting the potential impact of the eurozone crisis on North America?

LAWRENCE SUMMERS: She's not. There is the spectre of serious problems, and that could continue for some time. But a European crisis that primarily hurts Europe, that also hurts the United States, is a very different thing than an era of stagnation, which is what your resolution adopted. Maybe it would be helpful if those arguing the pessimistic side of the resolution could clarify whether it is their view that all is lost, that we've done vast amounts of policy and it's hopeless in the face of de-leveraging, as Mr. Rosenberg suggested, or whether our problems are eminently solvable, but we're unwilling to solve them, as Mr. Krugman suggests.

Those are rather different positions. My position, which is the same as Ms. Lagarde's position, and I think also Mr. Krugman's, is that these problems are solvable. Ms. Lagarde said what she said in the spirit of urging that these problems be solved. And while I'm sure the solution will be imperfect, I think that warnings of this kind are very salutary precisely because they prove to be self-denying prophecies and call forth action.

PAUL KRUGMAN: I do agree that these are very solvable problems, given the understanding and the will. That's my problem. We don't have those things. It's a little bit harder than Larry says. It's not just printing money. It's actually promising to keep that money out there after the economy has recovered. It's a trickier proposition than it might have seemed but, yes, a commitment to sustain monetary expansion might do it. The trouble is I see no prospect of it.

I think that Ian Bremmer has got this thing by exactly the wrong end of the beast, he has got it exactly upside down. We should not rejoice or feel optimistic about America because the rest of the world is doing even worse. That's not the way this thing works. The prospects for a lost decade in the United States are made more likely by the fact that so much of the rest of the world is doing badly. The European experience does hurt us. It doesn't help us. That's part of the point I was trying to make. Japan at least had the advantage of having a generally prosperous world to sell to; we do not.

And Larry, you're not quite right. It's true that a shock, a financial shock, by itself from Europe does not mean a lost decade, but it does tend to tip us further into that zone where there is a self-reinforcing downward spiral that keeps us trapped.

RUDYARD GRIFFITHS: Let's go to Ian, and then I'm going to get David to weigh in and then Larry, back to you. Ian, Paul says it's not about the world, it's not relative. It's about America.

IAN BREMMER: There's no question that the horrible economic situation in the world is going to have an impact on the United States. But the relative gain matters in terms of where you are going to put your money. Does it matter that millionaires in China, over 50 percent of them, want to live in the United States — not just send their kids over there, but actually live there? Yes, it does.

22

Does that attraction of entrepreneurship and talent make a difference to the United States? Of course it does.

I only had six minutes for my opening statement. We didn't talk about the fact that the single largest technological game-changer in the world, in my view, over the last few years is unconventional oil and gas, developed by American and Canadian entrepreneurs, these are American and Canadian multinational corporations. And now the United States is in vastly better shape in terms of a big energy game-changer. That's an enormous shift, and if you ask me where the next big thing is going to come from, I might bet a little less on the United States than I would have five years ago, but I'm still making the U.S. bet. Those are things that we can't just slough aside.

PAUL KRUGMAN: When the world loves the U.S. dollar, that is not helping us. We want a weak dollar. We want to export. The fact that people are piling up the U.S. dollar, the fact that people want to park their money in the United States, is not a positive in this situation. These are things that actually hurt the United States.

RUDYARD GRIFFITHS: David, come in on the European debt crisis, because some commentators have said that we have a lower debt to GDP ratio here in North America; less of our economy is made up of public expenditures. In other words, we're not going to have to spend a decade going through the painful debates, political and economic, that Europe's going to have to face. And that may be to our advantage.

DAVID ROSENBERG: It depends what debt you're looking at. If you're looking at total level of debt — and that's not where the problem is — if you add up corporate, household, and government debt in the United States, it's 350 percent of GDP. Does that make you feel comfortable? The OECD [Organisation for Economic Co-operation and Development] as a whole is up 375 percent, so the United States is really that materially below.

In answer to your question before, there is a solution to a credit collapse. Meanwhile, Europe's been working on one for twenty months. The United States has been working on one for basically three years, and the view somehow is that we're going to give more booze to the drunken sailor. We are not going to solve an existing credit crisis by creating more debt.

What happened in the United States is that by late '07, early '08, the U.S. consumer hit a wall. What happened amongst several European governments is that they hit a wall. So I guess if we're willing to agree, we can agree that the problem, globally, is one of excessive indebtedness. Then I'd like someone to enlighten me. What is the policy prescription?

One person's liability is somebody else's asset. Your liability is an asset at some financial institution, so explain to me how we're going to embark on this process of destroying debt because debt has to be destroyed. We finally hit the wall. When I ran around with Merrill Lynch for all those years and I had all my debt to GDP charts, all I ever heard was, "But it's not doing anything. You're just the boy who cried wolf." To which I replied,

"Well, remember, the wolf shows up at the end of the story." The wolf has shown up, and I'm hearing that there's actually an easy solution. We've had quite a long time to deal with the solution.

The problem is the law of unintended consequences; by destroying the debt you're creating winners and you're creating losers. If you're going to destroy the debt, you're going to have to somehow nationalize banks, or have the government help them recapitalize. Either that or you will have to inflate your way out of it by printing money.

RUDYARD GRIFFITHS: Nationalizing banks, Larry, that sounds a little extreme.

LAWRENCE SUMMERS: No, no. Look, we can come back to that if you want, but I just want to get some clarity on what we've been discussing. We've got a bit of a problem in that we've got two teams here but there's a little dissension within the teams. Paul and I agree that —

PAUL KRUGMAN: We do, which is why I'm so fascinated by your optimism.

LAWRENCE SUMMERS: I'm sorry?

PAUL KRUGMAN: Since we agree on the fundamentals, I'm a little baffled by your underlying position.

LAWRENCE SUMMERS: The central problem that is holding the American economy and the North American economy back is lack of demand. That is a problem that is very much made by man and can very much be solved by man. The central issues that go into solving it involve the proper use of fiscal policy, the proper use of monetary policy — both in the present and committed for the future, and with the proper reference to promote exports.

Paul and I might have some technical differences as to just how that might be done, but that is the centre of the problem and we have no disagreement there. The question is whether those relatively technical, incredibly important steps can be carried out in relatively short order. Principally, these steps have to do with monetary policy, and they are what make it appropriate to compare the United States' situation to what Japan's situation was at the beginning of the 1990s.

But I believe Japan faced a much more profound difficulty, a much larger bubble, and a huge set of deep structural problems around demography, insularity, and a lack of competition, all of which slowed it down in a way that has basically become permanent. There is no evidence that something like that is happening to the United States. That makes the historical nature of the situation in Japan — a country labelled the next superstate, which is now moving into decline — quite different from the situation in the United States. The United States is suffering from severe demand and financial problems to a lesser extent than the rest of the troubled world. Those are two very different situations. To recognize their difference is not to deny in any way the seriousness of the

U.S. situation, only to suggest that it is not the kind of U-turn in history from ascent to descent that took place in Japan after 1989.

IAN BREMMER: When you talk about Japan and you talk about an era, you talk about something that's become very fashionable in Washington circles these days — decline. Declinism, declinist. You can't take a one-year, a two-year, a granular policy perspective, asking yourself, what will or what won't Congress do on the deficit today? You have to look at the long-term position of the United States in the world. Is China becoming number one? Is that something to bet on? It's not a question of whether or not China is going to hurt the United States tomorrow. It's a question of who is going to be number one. Where are we going? American demographics are fundamentally strong. The population is growing, and immigration is reasonably healthy. It is a fairly creative country, right? You compare that with Japan's growth, and give me a break. You compare it with Europe's growth, and you realize they are going nowhere on this front. You compare it with China, and population growth is becoming vastly more problematic there.

You've got a world that's industrializing with hundreds and hundreds of millions of people coming into the middle class. They need food. Who's got it? The United States. They are net exporters of calories. They are the world's largest producers in terms of things like corn and grain. Consider the long term. When you think in terms of eras, we're not talking about hedge funds

anymore, we're talking about where you and your kids
are going to be. And it seems to me that it is a no-brainer.
I'm as stunned as Paul is that these guys are not on our
side. I don't see where else there is to go.

RUDYARD GRIFFITHS: We've got three slides on Japan to
give the audience a sense of what an era of decline looks
like. Slide one is the Japanese GDP going back to 1985,
the big spike-down obviously is the financial crisis, but
then it's back down to zero.

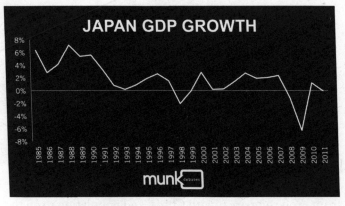

Source: World Bank

In slide two we see interest rates over a long period
bumping along close to zero.

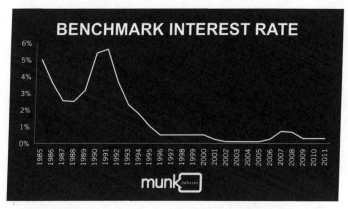

Source: TradingEconomics.com; Bank of Japan

The final graphic (slide three) represents public indebtedness.

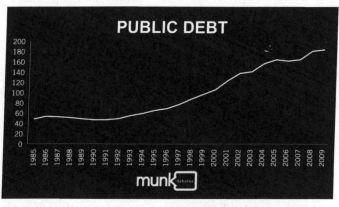

Source: OECD

Tell us why you think that the Japanese experience is more analogous than less to what we face. That seems to be the core of this debate so far.

PAUL KRUGMAN: So far, the United States looks like the beginning of that series of slides, except more compressed in time; it is kind of Japan's lost decade on Internet time, if you will.

I think there's fundamental confusion going on, there are two different issues. One is an issue of long-term secular growth, creativity, and of course demographics. Sure, the United States has the advantage on those. If ten years from now the United States is exactly comparable to Japan, except with a higher GDP that's entirely accounted for by higher population growth, if our per capita GDP does what Japan's does, would we think we had escaped Japan's fate? I don't think so. We would say that we had experienced a lost decade just like theirs. That's not the issue, nor is our place in the world the question. The question is, are we going to be stuck in a state of depressed demand of the kind that Larry has talked about?

Larry and I agree that that is what has been happening, and I think David agrees as well. We agree that a lot of the things that we've talked about, creativity and dynamism, for example, are wonderful. Do they solve our problems? There are stories which lead us to believe that they might, but I always look back to the 1930s, when the United States was, even more than it is now, the cutting-edge technological country. The United States was more dynamic than any other country, and yet we were stuck in the Great Depression. It was only a very large public works program otherwise known as World War II that took us out.

Politically, you want to consider the long term. I come from the perspective that the U.S. political system has changed fundamentally. We are not the country we were. The days when twenty senators from both parties, evenly divided, could get together and agree on a set of reasonable, moderate measures are long gone. We're a deeply polarized country; we have a dysfunctional political system in a way that it never was. We didn't use to be a country where nothing could be passed without the votes of sixty senators. We are now; neither party is likely to have sixty senators any time in the foreseeable future, and nothing can be done about that.

So, sure, I think Larry and I agree almost entirely on the economics, on what needs to be done; but I have a deep pessimism about the state of the United States as a political entity. I don't see anything that makes me hopeful for the next few years, at least.

LAWRENCE SUMMERS: Winston Churchill famously said that the United States always does the right thing, but only after exhausting the alternatives. The theory of universal gridlock is tricky. Certainly there are many alternatives that I would have strongly preferred, starting with more fiscal stimulus, that Congress was unwilling to give in the last two years. This gridlock will continue, judging by the current political debate. But those who say that the United States is now hopelessly gridlocked do need to remember this fact: every political scientist and historian who has looked at the question of how much consequential legislation was passed in 2009 and 2010 versus any other period has concluded that there is a good debate to be had about 2009 and 2010 versus 1965 and 1966. There is no comparable period of productivity and legislation in forty years, and there are many who think you have to go back to 1933 and 1934 to find a period when an equal amount of consequential legislation passed.

So, yes, is there gridlock with respect to some issues that I think are hugely important right now? Yes, there is. Does that mean that the system is fundamentally blocked for the long term? I think the magnitude of what has happened must be considered. I think you also have to look to differences in private sector initiatives. While Rudyard was introducing the people who brought us this forum — Peter and Melanie Munk — the thought came into my head that this kind of spur to public debate to solve problems is a North American strength, and it is not an important feature of life in other parts of the world. As we assess our prospects we need to look to all the strengths of societies.

RUDYARD GRIFFITHS: Let's change gears before we go to questions from the audience. Ian, I want to start with you. Let's talk about the Occupy Wall Street movement. It's here in Canada, too, and one of the protesters' major grievances is the inequality of wealth that we see on this continent. And I think that's a grievance that is shared by a lot of people on both sides of the political spectrum. So why isn't that really an Achilles heel for North America?

IAN BREMMER: Why wasn't Hurricane Katrina an Achilles heel? I went to Tulane University, down in New Orleans. It is horrifying what happened there. We said, "Never again," and we keep saying it. The fact is that the United States is an extraordinarily, exceptionally resilient country. Why didn't the elections in 2000, which 50 percent of the population believed were fraudulent, cause chaos in the streets? What if that had happened in Indonesia or Ukraine? It did happen in Ukraine, actually, and there was a very different response.

It's because the United States has extraordinary depths of political resilience and stability. In that regard we're similar to Japan, there is no question. Think about the Fukushima Daiichi nuclear disaster, the resilience is there. But unlike Japan, the United States also has the potential to grow and create, and all the rest.

So the Occupy Wall Street movement is an embarrassment for the United States, there is no question. But the fact that we are debating as vigorously as we are and that these movements are happening across the country and that they matter, is a great thing. One reason the five-dollar fee for debit transactions for ATM cards — which was not exactly good timing on the part of the banks — got pulled apart was because you had folks on the streets saying, "We're not going to take this sort of thing anymore." And the banks said, "Wow, this may be bad for us."

I think that is a real strength of the United States. I don't think it's a weakness. But clearly it needs to be addressed.

RUDYARD GRIFFITHS: Paul, you've written extensively about this.

PAUL KRUGMAN: It is possible to have full employment producing luxury goods. But I think inequality plays an indirect role in a lot of our political polarization. A lot of the pulling apart of our political system appears to be related to inequality. Political scientists have shown that those two track each other pretty closely. I also think a lot of the way we got into this mess was through reckless deregulation, through a failure to rein in the financial sector — a sort of determined forgetting of the lessons of the 1930s, which never at any point worked very well.

We never actually had a particularly successful economy. Yet there was this impression in Washington and in New York among people who had influence that it was working just great when actually it was only working great for them. The thirty years following the big change in America, the big shift to the right, were actually not a good time for American middle-class families, but they were great for the top 0.1 percent. I think inequality has in fact warped the perspective of our policy elites, and continues to do so.

I don't think inequality is crucial, though. I think the United States and Japan are similar and our macroeconomic experiences are alarmingly similar, though the Japanese managed to do it without all of this inequality. So, yes, we don't have their weaknesses, but we have weaknesses of our own, and inequality is one of them.

RUDYARD GRIFFITHS: David, what's your take on this? Does inequality lead to the potential for political crisis in North America similar to what we are seeing in Europe? Could we ever see people in the streets like we do in Greece or Rome?

DAVID ROSENBERG: Well, I don't want to go that far, but it does lead to social instability. Larry Summers mentioned the deficiency of aggregate demand. Our opponents haven't mentioned the word "de-leveraging," they haven't mentioned how housing fits in and what the root cause of the demand deficiency has been. If we don't agree on the root cause, then we're not going to come to a solution.

There are about 20 million Americans that are upside down on their mortgages, and if they get a job offer in another city they can't leave unless they write their lender a cheque. So that is just one example among many of how housing and credit have played into unemployment.

When you have a situation where almost half of unemployed people have been searching fruitlessly for work for at least six months, you know what is going to happen. When you have a youth unemployment rate in the United States of 24 percent, an adult male unemployment rate of 8.5 percent — and without a college education it is 14 percent — you know what is going to happen with these people. Everything, ultimately, will come right down to unemployment, so there are a lot of disenfranchised individuals with a lot of idle time and perhaps not a lot of prospects. We're past the peak of the stimulus cycle, whether it pertains to federal fiscal policy or monetary policy.

I think Larry might agree with me — I mean, we're basically writing different chapters of the book on the age of de-leveraging, and I don't want to sound alarmist, I'm not talking about riots in the streets, but the longer there is a serious unemployment problem in the United States the more you risk social instability.

Keep in mind that we're not even in a technical recession. We're supposedly in the third year of a statistical recovery. And it's not just a 9 percent unemployment rate when you count all the underemployment — there are so many people working part-time that used to work full-time. The real unemployment rate, as you well know, is over 16 percent. The longer that lingers, the greater the risk of some sort of social instability.

I don't know if there is really a consistent message from this Occupy Wall Whatever–Street movement, but I'll tell you that there is one thing that resonates through the group: I think it's a backlash against excessive CEO pay in the United States. The fact that there are people running banks who are forced out by the board and they get this enormous pay package at a time when more than 40 million people are receiving food stamps, well, that sort of leaves a bad taste in people's mouths. So I think it comes down more to the golden parachutes. As far as I'm concerned, if there's a common thread, that's what it is.

RUDYARD GRIFFITHS: Larry, go ahead, and then Paul.

LAWRENCE SUMMERS: The trend towards greater inequality is a highly problematic thing. Too much of it has to do with people who have successfully managed to get the government to directly or indirectly give them resources. There's much that needs to be done to remedy that, starting with more progressive taxation and a variety of regulatory changes.

On the other hand, let's remember there is another aspect to this, although it is not by any means the whole story. It may not even be half the story, but it is worth keeping in mind. Suppose the United States had thirty more people like Steve Jobs. Would that be good or would that be bad? I think it would be good, but the level of inequality in the United States would be significantly higher. So, we do need to recognize that a component of this inequality is the other side of successful entrepreneurship, and that is surely something we want to encourage. Too much of the inequality we are seeing comes from other things, but let's not forget that some of the great fortunes have been made doing things that have had very substantial benefits for large numbers of North Americans and people around the world.

PAUL KRUGMAN: That is correct, but almost none of the top 1 percent is like that. Some are very important people, but there are very few of them. I want to say, in case it wasn't clear, that I think the Occupy Wall Street has been an entirely positive development. It's been entirely salutary. People ask, "Where does it go from here?" It has already changed the discussion in a favourable way.

We've stopped talking about inflicting pain and started talking more about creating jobs. Occupy Wall Street has actually moved me marginally towards Larry's position, giving me some hope that maybe, maybe, there are resources in the American psyche that will get us out of this mess. But then I turn on the TV and watch another GOP debate and I change my mind.

RUDYARD GRIFFITHS: We have some interesting people in the audience who have a lot of experience with these issues, and I'm going to go to some of them for their questions. The first person I want to call on is someone who lives and breathes the cross-border economy every day. He is the president and CEO of the sixth largest bank in North America, Ed Clark.

ED CLARK: I'm not sure now whether we've got two teams or four individuals, so I'm going to try and tease that out of you. Assuming you're in the 95 percent and you're willing to change your mind, if you came to the view of your opponents in this debate, what policy prescription would you do differently?

RUDYARD GRIFFITHS: Ian, I'm going to ask you to kick us off.

IAN BREMMER: Well, I suppose it would become a little more urgent. I don't suppose it's that the policies would change, but the willingness to kick the can down the road changes. I mean the Americans, the Europeans, the

Chinese, the Japanese, they are all kicking a can down the road. Number one, you need to hit the can; number two, you need to have road. The United States is consistently kicking the can, as opposed to the Europeans, who came very close to missing the can altogether the last couple of weeks.

Secondly, you've got a lot of road, and actually you've got folks out there that have a brick wall in front of them, and they're not drilling. I think if I were more convinced by their position I'd be more concerned about the urgency of things like massive infrastructure spending, change and improvement in educational policy — especially at the younger ages, because that's a generational issue and you've got to work on that right away.

I still support the policy, but how urgent is it? Is it okay that we are waiting until 2013? I understand that Paul gets upset whenever he sees the GOP. That's actually not a constructive position in the sense that the GOP does reflect half of the American population. I don't get upset when I see political parties. I want to see governance. One thing that is interesting to note when we look at 2012 is that we're much more likely to see more governance.

It seems to me, looking at the trends, that the House is going to go Republican, the Senate is going to go more Republican, and the presidential race is actually swaying a little more towards Barack Obama than Mitt Romney at this point, but it could go either way. Either of those two outcomes from my perspective indicates that there is likely to be more governance, though Paul may not like the governance in question, and more policy than there has been over the last few years. Especially since it would be President Obama's second term and he needs a legacy. He has to compromise; there's only one way to do it.

So the question is, can we wait until 2013 to move that ball, or do we have to get started now?

LAWRENCE SUMMERS: In a democracy, often fear does the work of reason. I think the kind of concerns that have been expressed during this debate are very constructive because they call forth the kinds of policy responses that we need, which I believe will be forthcoming sooner or later. And that means that this will be remembered as having been a hugely significant and painful cyclical episode in American history, but not the equivalent of the decline of Britain, and not the equivalent of the historical change in Japan's role in the world.

If I really believed that [the United States was in decline], I would think that the United States needed to profoundly reassess its approach to global leadership in the context of being able to afford much less. I don't believe that the United States needs to do that, and I believe it would be enormously dangerous if the United States were to do that, both for American interests, for global peace, and for freedom around the world.

So it is appropriate to worry terribly about the various concerns that we have discussed, but to write off the American future by declaring that we are in an era — not a decade — of stagnation seems to me to risk a self-fulfilling prophecy of a most dangerous sort. But that is the direction in which I believe the United States would have to move if these views were accepted.

PAUL KRUGMAN: Given my perspective, I'm not sure the question quite makes sense. The reason that we face the prospect of a decade or more — I don't know how long an era is, but a long stretch — of very bad times is precisely because we are unlikely to put the right policies in place. I'm very much of the view that we could end this quite quickly.

I don't know if people have heard my line that if we discovered an external threat, if we were told the space aliens were getting ready to invade and we needed to prepare for it by spending a lot of money, we'd be out of this thing in eighteen months. And then if we discovered that aliens didn't really exist, fine, we would have solved the problem. But that scenario is not going to happen. What I advise for policy is almost exactly what Larry advises for policy — radical monetary and fiscal stimulus until we're out of this — but I see nothing in the political spectrum that leads me to think it's going to happen.

Let me say one other thing. We talk about the history of the United States, and the history of the world, and during the course of history nobody has ever done what needed to be done. No country has ever successfully responded to the aftermath of a major financial crisis with an effective monetary and stimulus package. The countries that have got out of financial crises since World War II have done so with export-led recoveries.

They have all been the kinds of recoveries that are not available to us.

The United States did not do it in the 1930s. There are a lot of favourable comparisons between President Obama and President Franklin Delano Roosevelt in terms of what they accomplished in their first two years, but FDR did not get the United States out of the Depression. It was Japan's Prime Minister Hideki Tojo who got us out. So we're not only demanding optimism, we're demanding that you believe that America is going to find a way to do something that nobody has ever done before.

RUDYARD GRIFFITHS: David?

DAVID ROSENBERG: It might be time to take off the gloves, which isn't my style, but Larry said in April 2010 that the economy had achieved escape velocity. Since that time the Federal Reserve has cut their macro-forecast five times. So this is an unpredictable and extremely volatile economic backdrop. We're already in an era of extraordinarily weak economic growth. The question is whether the era is going to persist. Employment in the United States is the same level today that it was in June 2000. There's been no change in eleven years. The S&P 500 is at the same level it was in January 1999. Home prices are at the same level they were in 2003. Real personal income is at the same level it was in 2005. So I don't know how you want to define an era, or what is long-term, or secular, but we have had the same statistics for somewhere between six and twelve years.

I'm glad Ian brought up Canada. Canada went through a fiscal crisis of its own in the 1990s and we brought in a Goods and Services Tax and a sales tax, and the government that got elected in 1993 campaigned that it would do away with the Goods and Services Tax. And here we are today, and the tax still raises about 35 billion dollars into government coffers. If the American public were to grab onto the fact that there are all these loopholes and writeoffs that create misallocation of resources, well, there's a trillion dollars right there that could have gone into federal revenues.

There are other things. For example, Ian brought up natural gas. Now, you can't turn back the clock, but what about how President Eisenhower was able to wrap a whole job creation machine around hundreds of thousands of miles of highway infrastructure? Look what that did to labour mobility rates in the United States, to long-term rates of return on the capital that was invested, and to productivity growth. Currently we have a president who got elected by talking about the need for a coherent energy policy. Well, where is it? Look at the abundance of cheap natural gas. I don't want to get into an environmental debate, but a coherent energy policy would be great.

Those are the things I would do in terms of the tax system, and in terms of energy policy tying into job creation — because it is very labour-intensive — and then, thirdly, I'd come back to the de-leveraging cycle. How does the government ease the process when you have almost 20 million Americans upside down on mortgages for their homes? That is inherently unstable from a social standpoint, and from an economic standpoint. We have to find a way to give these people back the equity in their homes. How do you do that? Equity means a writeoff for the banking system, and while I'm not saying we should nationalize the banks, maybe they'll have to go through another period of recapitalization. Maybe they'll need the assistance of the public sector. I don't think that we're going to get the ball moving in this economy until we get an improvement in housing. And when I say housing I'm not only talking about housing starts. I'm talking about putting a floor to home prices, and without mentioning moral hazard — because we swept that under the carpet three years ago — we have to find a way to give equity back in people's hands.

RUDYARD GRIFFITHS: Let's go to another audience question. It's my pleasure to call on my former colleague, Business News Network anchor Kim Parlee, for her question.

KIM PARLEE: Selfishly, I'd like to turn the conversation to Canada if I could. What should Canada do today, given events in the United States and Europe, to either protect itself or take advantage of some growth that might be happening?

RUDYARD GRIFFITHS: I'll ask each of you for your big Canadian idea. I'll start with you, Ian.

IAN BREMMER: I'd build up the polar north. I'd bet on climate change; no one is going to be able to fix that. I'd go short on Panama and long on Canada. Canada has icebreakers. America doesn't do that.

I go to Calgary a fair amount and the question I always get there is, "When is the United States going to start getting freaked out about the Chinese coming in and investing equity stakes and all the rest?" And the answer is, "Soon." So, be proactive. You've got the Keystone XL pipeline that just got pushed back, but it will reappear after the U.S. elections. This is a great opportunity for Canadians to make sure that they're diversified and can take advantage of the other countries out there that are growing and want access to Canadian commodities. But don't get in bed with them. The Brazilians understand this in relation to land. There are strings attached. There is conditionality that comes with entering into an agreement with China, just like there is conditionality that comes to agreements with the United States. You're not going to like that conditionality, either. You're not Australia, which is all China all the time. But take advantage of that hedge and get out in front.

RUDYARD GRIFFITHS: Larry?

LAWRENCE SUMMERS: Canada is part of a world that is slower, which means that you're going to have to create more demand. That applies to your monetary policies. That applies to fiscal policies. That applies to financial policies. Recognize that you are going to need to sustain demand, and that there are risks in terms of what the global economy can bring in terms of demand.

RUDYARD GRIFFITHS: Our interest rates are not quite at zero yet, so we've got a little bit of room.

PAUL KRUGMAN: That plays into what I was going to say — hang onto your independent currency. What a great thing it is . . .

RUDYARD GRIFFITHS: No to the "amero."

PAUL KRUGMAN: That's right, no to the amero. Keep your own dollar. What a great thing it is to keep your flexibility. The two standout economies in the advanced world in terms of getting through this crisis relatively unscathed are those of Canada and Sweden. Both countries are on the edge of a large currency union but have kept their own currency, which has given them crucial flexibility.

RUDYARD GRIFFITHS: David, as the Canadian on the panel, you're going to have to deliver here.

DAVID ROSENBERG: What's the old real estate saying? "Location, location, location." We have a great location right next to the United States, so we can limit any potential economic damage by ensuring that there is substantial room on the federal fiscal side to stimulate if need be. If this turns into a global recession, everyone is going to be affected. I often hear that Canada hasn't diversified enough from the United States, but in some ways I think we have, especially when it comes to our capital markets. Half of the stock market in this country is hitched to commodities, and that has more to do with Asia and China, because the United States is not the marginal buyer of commodities and hasn't been for decades. The United States is the marginal buyer of services.

We're not totally detached from the United States, but here again the proof of the pudding is in the eating. The United States had a recession in 2001 and Canada did not have a recession in 2001 or 2002. What is interesting is that the U.S. recession started in December 2007, and very quickly the U.S. stock market went down 20 percent, but Canada's market went up 20 percent to a new high. We didn't start a recession until about seven or eight months later. And it was really only when it became a global recession, when it stopped being a U.S. recession, that it affected Canada. China went down for the count and it really opened up the trap door. But it is interesting that we have made great strides towards weaning ourselves off the full effects of the recession in the United States.

RUDYARD GRIFFITHS: Our next question comes from a very well-known Canadian. He is the author of several books, a professor at the University of Toronto, and a former leader of the Liberal Party of Canada, Michael Ignatieff.

MICHAEL IGNATIEFF: I want to focus discussion on one issue that has recurred throughout this debate, and that is political gridlock in Washington. There seems to be some disagreement about how serious an impediment to growth and recovery it is. What would be the advice of the panel to the incoming U.S. president in November 2012, whoever it is, to make the political system work more effectively?

PAUL KRUGMAN: A lot of it depends on which party the president belongs to. If the president is a Republican, I think he will have no trouble pushing through a lot of really destructive ideas. If President Obama is re-elected, he's going to have to use every parliamentary trick and every administrative trick available to him. If the Democrats do regain control of the House and retain a majority of the Senate — which is within the realm of the possible — then the president is going to have to use whatever tools are available to find a way to break that sixty-vote rule.

If the Democrats fail to control one or both houses of Congress, the president is going to have to use the powers of the presidency to bypass Congress. There is only so much a president can do. The gridlock in the U.S. system is not something that's small. It's not something that's petty. We've got a deep philosophical difference between the two parties. They fundamentally disagree on not only how things work, but on morality, on what is right and wrong. The idea that somehow you can finesse those differences and that if you say the right words they will go away is naive.

So the president elected in 2012 is going to·have to

find a way to get stuff done despite that, which is going to be very, very hard.

IAN BREMMER: It's a big question. Let me try to give you the big picture on it. As a world power, the United States has never been considered the same way other countries have, either by itself or by others. It's the indispensable nation, the exceptional nation. And I think whether the next president is Mitt Romney or Barack Obama, they need to understand both sides of that coin. That's the way they can lead. Fundamentally, all of this amounts to leadership. You need a president that is seen as a leader, by their colleagues and by their opposition. When Bill Clinton was president, people felt that he was a leader whether or not they agreed with him, or liked him.

I think Obama has done a great job of understanding how the United States has eroded a lot of its credibility — whether it's human rights, rule of law, free markets, accounting firms, or gold standards. But he's done a really bad job of understanding American exceptionalism.

Romney, on the other hand — and let's face it, Romney is going to be elected, there's not much choice — has, in his foreign policy speeches and his big-think speeches, focused on American indispensability, the Reagan era, and exceptionalism. But he has paid absolutely no attention to everything that has happened in the past ten years that has eroded that exceptionalism.

They have to meet on this. Anyone that wants to be the president of the "free world" — we don't hear that term very much anymore — has to find a way to bridge those two things. The president has to know not only how to make America great again, but the president has to know how to make politicians around the world understand that America is great again. We have to get that right.

RUDYARD GRIFFITHS: David, you lived and worked in the United States and it's a big part of your business now. What is your answer for the improvement of the political system in the United States?

DAVID ROSENBERG: If Hank Paulson could go down on one knee and beg Nancy Pelosi to pass TARP for a second time, I imagine anything is possible.[2] That is my reason for hope. My concern is that it is hard to believe that what happened back then is a Republican president, that was actually a lame duck president, worked effectively with Congress to get something done. Unfortunately, it took a crisis to push them into considerable action. And maybe we have to live through a crisis again to get the people in Washington moving in the right direction.

RUDYARD GRIFFITHS: Larry, last word to you.

---

[2] In September 2008, during tension-filled negotiations to get the Troubled Asset Relief Program (TARP) through the U.S. House of Representatives, Treasury Secretary Henry "Hank" Paulson got down on bended knee to ask House Speaker Nancy Pelosi, a Democrat, for her party's support. The $700 billion bank bailout bill was eventually signed into law by President George W. Bush the following month.

LAWRENCE SUMMERS: It obviously makes a difference whether it's a Republican president or if President Obama is re-elected. Obviously, I have a very strong view about which would be better for America. But forced to answer the question in general terms, I'd answer it this way: our employment, our output, and our macroeconomic problems are of a magnitude that everyone has to move beyond. It's what I call "now more than ever-ism." There is a strong tendency for both parties to have agendas and to apply those agendas to the context of the moment. For example, certain members of the Republican Party always think it's time to cut capital gains taxes. Sometimes it's because the United States is in a recession and we need more demand, and sometimes it's because we have a boom and we need more supply, but the policy recommendation is constant. There are also those who have other agendas: whether it's heavy involvement of the government in green energy or other areas that they regard as necessary when there is a recession, or as a necessary antidote policy when there's a boom. The prospects of coming together on effective solutions are enhanced if we can define the central problem not as "finding everything America needs" but as responding to the seriousness of the current recession. My guess is that Keynes actually had this right. Keynes said that it was very important to raise demand along the lines of fiscal and monetary policies. He also spoke of the importance of pursuing policies that would enhance business confidence because that would increase investment. If we can borrow those two ideas, I think the next presidential term can be one of significant improvement for the American economy.

RUDYARD GRIFFITHS: It's now time for the closing statements. We'll go in the opposite order of the opening remarks, so, Ian Bremmer, you're up first.

IAN BREMMER: Thank you very much. This has been fun and instructive. I want to say first that I didn't hear anyone responding negatively to the notion that Canada is in very good shape. I would bear in mind that we are talking about North America as you vote. Secondly, Larry and I have put a lot of issues on the table; we were talking about American capacity over the long term. And while I've heard a lot of concerns about American gridlock — concerns I feel we've rebutted — I didn't hear much response on some of these big issues that drive American growth in the long term.

Philanthropy matters. Go to sub-Saharan Africa. The Gates Foundation is all over there and they're planting what look like American flags for the local Africans. They perceive China very differently in sub-Saharan Africa. Does that make any difference in the long term? Absolutely. Who else is doing this? Broadly speaking, we're not seeing that from the emerging markets that are doing so much of the marginal driving.

We also talked about the importance of demographics. We haven't mentioned women, but women graduating from university in the United States represent 51 percent of the workforce. They've got opportunities in the United States they don't have in a lot of other places. I go to Japan; I have forty meetings and the women there serve me tea, but they're not playing a productive role in the Japanese economy. They're not playing as productive a role in the European economy. That's an issue where the United States has an advantage, and it's going to develop a larger advantage.

I talked about energy. I talked about food. But I think the big thing to focus on is the next new thing, and we don't know what it is yet. We get surprised by new things a lot. Over the course of the last hundred years, look at the innovation and look at where the innovation has come from. Look at how innovations have changed the way we think about the world. Not just Steve Jobs. Look at the Arab Spring, look at the impact that may have on China over time.

But the big new things are coming from the United States, and the reason they are coming from the United States is not only because it's the world's largest market, though that matters. It's not only because we have a lot of capital and smart people, though that matters. The big new things come from the United States because when Americans are educated they're taught to question things. That's the reason there are a lot of people who finish college, who didn't do so well or who even drop out, but start up major multinational corporations that end up changing the future of the world. That's not happening in Europe, Japan, or China.

I feel great about Sweden. I was there recently, and the weather was nice. I had a great time. I feel good about

Singapore. I like a lot of Scandinavia. I like Canada. But of anything of size out there, if you have to make bets, and all of us here do, the United States is where you go.

RUDYARD GRIFFITHS: David, you're up next.

DAVID ROSENBERG: It's been fun and entertaining. I have great respect for my opponents, and frankly, I just want to win this debate.

I have a dual role at Gluskin Sheff: I am the chief economist and the chief strategist. When people ask the strategist, "Where's the market going?" I tell them where the market is going. When they ask, "Where's the economy going?" I have to heed the message that the market is giving me.

One of the charts that we looked at before was on interest rates. What does it mean to me, an economist, or to anyone in the room for that matter — my opponents and Paul Krugman — when the three-month Treasury bill is one basis point above zero? What does it mean when the yield on the five-year Treasury note is below 1 percent? What does that mean? What does it mean when the yield on the ten-year Treasury note is a two? That is exactly the same yield-curve that Japan had circa 1999, a full decade after their initial detonation.

What were the money market and the bond market telling us about the outlook on the economy? And the answer is two words: fundamentally weak.

There's another aspect to the Treasury curve. If you haven't heard of it, it's called the TIPS market, or

Treasury Inflation Protected Securities. It is a proxy for real interest rates, and real interest rates in turn are a proxy for real economic growth. Today and pretty well for every single day in November the yield on the five-year TIPS, which is a real rate, has been negative 1 percent. So I will let the market do the talking. Do you know that exactly ten years ago the yield on the TIPS was sitting at just below 2 percent? At that point the ten-year average growth rate was 3.5 percent and the ten-year TIP was 1.7 percent. That's exactly what GDP growth has been for the last ten years, Mr. Bond. Thank you very much.

RUDYARD GRIFFITHS: Lawrence Summers, your concluding remarks, please.

LAWRENCE SUMMERS: David, you referenced where we were ten years ago. At that time I was just stepping down as Treasury Secretary, and the United States of America was paying down debt on a record scale and its economy had created jobs more rapidly than during any other decade. Your economics on interest rates were very surprising to me. The European Central Bank, motivated by exactly what you described, raised interest rates six months ago. That is a significant reason why Europe is in crisis now. The best news we could get about the global economy in the next six months would come from interest rates falling to American levels.

I want to make two points. The first is this: if you look at a broad range of human experience, you can rarely go wrong with the maxim that things are not as bad as you think they are when you think they are bad, and that things are not as good as you think they are when you think they are good. That is the mistake people made in perpetuating the bubble, and that is the mistake they are making now.

Think about how inconceivable it would have seemed five years ago, ten years ago, that the United States would elect an African-American president. Think about how inconceivable it would have seemed during the Cold War that that war would end peaceably. Think about how inconceivable it would have seemed that the United States, which was being written off as a global competitor, would succeed as it did during the 1990s.

Paul and I at least agree that these problems are solvable. I can't tell you exactly when it will happen, but no one who has watched political life can deny that the transition from inconceivable to inevitable can be very rapid. I believe these problems will be solved.

Second thing I would say is that if you adopt this resolution — a resolution that writes off the prospects of the United States — then you are contributing to a pessimism that as a self-fulfilling prophecy can be, and I believe will be, catastrophic not just for North America, but for the world. These problems can be solved, and they will be solved.

RUDYARD GRIFFITHS: Paul Krugman, you have the final word.

PAUL KRUGMAN: Larry began his opening remarks with one of my favourite quotes from John Maynard Keynes in 1931, saying that we have magneto problems. That is one of my favourite quotes, and I've never entirely forgiven *X-Men* for corrupting it and polluting it. What Keynes meant, of course, was that this is a problem that doesn't require that you change everything, but that there is only a small part of the system that has gone wrong and so it is fixable. Larry and I certainly believe that what we have is fixable. We have magneto problems. We have trouble with a fundamentally technical issue.

But there is another way to take that quote, and that is if you don't fix your magneto problem, if you don't fix what has gone wrong, nothing else that is good about the car is going to make any difference, or can make it go. It can have the most powerful engine, the most wonderful styling, and still, if you don't fix those magneto problems, this car is not going to go anywhere.

What I heard a lot from the con side during this debate was about how wonderful a country America is. And it is a wonderful country. I'm supposed to believe that, and I actually do. I think it is the world's greatest country. I think it has so many things, including creativity, flexibility, and innovation. All of those things are wonderful, but none of them solve the magneto problems. None of that solves the problem of inadequate demand.

So the question has to be, do you see a way to get this car going? I have not heard anything that tells me that there is any realistic prospect; certainly not next year or the year after, and not until there is a fundamental shift in our political climate and our political alignment that says we are actually going to do those things that need to be done.

Larry's final remarks are interesting. Should one not say something pessimistic, even if you possibly believe it, because it might come true? That is a fairly real issue that comes up in my current second job. I hear quite a lot — mostly from the Europeans but also from Americans — of people saying, "You know, even if you are pessimistic, you really shouldn't be saying these things because people read your columns and it's going to frighten people," and so forth. You can't live that way. That is wrong. You have to tell the truth, and the truth is that we have a fixable problem, but a political system and a political alignment that shows absolutely no willingness to fix that problem for quite a few years to come.

Summary: The pre-debate vote was 56 percent in favour of the resolution and 26 percent against, and 18 percent were undecided. The final vote showed a disappearance of the undecided voters, with 55 percent in favour of the resolution and 45 percent against. Given the shift in votes, the victory goes to the team arguing against the resolution, Lawrence Summers and Ian Bremmer.

PAUL KRUGMAN IN CONVERSATION
WITH BRIAN MILNER

BRIAN MILNER: Professor Krugman, during the debate tonight you took the position that the United States is heading into a long swoon, along Japanese lines, with a stagnant economy, very weak growth, and lots more problems. I wonder if you can expand a bit on that and why you have that kind of view.

PAUL KRUGMAN: The first thing to say is that we are already four years into this. We are four years since the beginning of the great recession. So it's not as if the notion of the United States being in a slump for a long period of time is hypothetical — that might happen — and there is no hint in the day-to-day of a rapid recovery. So, looking at history, you'd be hard put to make the case that we're not going to have a very extended period of slump. Basically, we are making all of the same mistakes. We've made all the mistakes that countries hit by severe financial crises characteristically make. They respond with inadequate stimulus, they pull back on the stimulus too soon, they get nervous about inflation, even though inflation's not the problem, and we're doing nothing that would turn this thing around. I'm not a fatalist, I don't believe that nothing could be done. We could end this quickly if we had forceful, effective policy with a strong political consensus behind it, but obviously that's not the situation.

BRIAN MILNER: We've had all of this even though we've had Ben Bernanke, a Fed chairman who was very sensitive to these issues. He has warned us about this for many years. Does this mean that the Fed really has done all it can and that the rest has to be on the fiscal side?

PAUL KRUGMAN: Not necessarily, although I'd feel a lot more comfortable about any recovery efforts if they were backed by a strong fiscal side as well, but what turns out, is that for the Fed to be effective it would have to do something that is more radical than Bernanke is willing to contemplate, or is at least willing to publicly contemplate given that he doesn't have his board behind him. Ben Bernanke thought a lot about this eleven years ago, as did I, and as did some others. His view was that the Fed could get enough traction, even in these conditions, by buying unconventional assets, by expanding its balance sheet buying long-term bonds, and so on, which is in fact what it has done, as quantitative easing. But even at the time I thought he was exaggerating how much traction he'd get. And, in any case, the size of the slump, and the size of the problem, has dwarfed anything that he, or I, was contemplating back then, and so the Fed could do something, perhaps, but it would have to be much bigger, much bolder, much more radical than anyone seems willing to contemplate at this point.

BRIAN MILNER: If you had a hand on the levers of economic power right now in Washington what would you do differently?

PAUL KRUGMAN: Waiving aside politics, we need a second large stimulus. This time focused on government spending and infrastructure, but also a lot of aid to state and local governments, because we've laid off about 300,000 school teachers, as that aid faded out. And then, at the same time, we need a monetary policy that is first of all supportive of that, we need plenty of monetary expansion as it's happening, plus a commitment to keep the party going, even after the economy has started to recover, to allow some rise in the inflation rate. Or allow nominal GDP to actually target a nominal GDP level that is substantially higher than the current projections, so that we get all of the cylinders firing. So we have an immediate direct push on demand from government spending, and a credible promise that the economy is going to be strong. And, by the way, if you sit on cash it's going to lose some of its value, which will get the private sector firing as well. The Great Depression ended because the war indirectly created that kind of environment — expansionary fiscal policy, expansionary monetary policy, and the expectation of future expansion, and that's what we need right now.

BRIAN MILNER: Would you still take on a deficit by eliminating the tax cuts? Would you put in new tax increases of any kind or would you look at a national sales tax?

PAUL KRUGMAN: Well this is stuff that you ideally do after the economy is recovered, but given the political economy, I think raising high-end taxes is not such a terrible thing. But certainly we need to undo the Bush tax cuts eventually. The economy did fine in the 1990s, and we need that revenue. It's probably not enough. If you take a longer term, even with highly effective cost control on health care, you need significant additional revenue. And I'm willing to go for a national sales tax as the sources of that additional revenue.

BRIAN MILNER: Do you get a sense that American people are more disposed to trying these things than their own political leaders at this point?

PAUL KRUGMAN: It is a question of how seriously you take people's answers in polls. For what it's worth, the public is quite favourably disposed towards higher taxes for upper income Americans. Actually, even a plurality of Republicans seems to favour that. The public is confused about the stimulus short-term measures, which is understandable. It's not easy to understand it, and there is a cacophony of voices. But, if I look at the political spectrum, it seems to me that what's regarded as the political centre in Washington, appears to be a little bit to the right of the average self-identified Republican in the polls, so there is something very strange going on.

BRIAN MILNER: So, this Tea Party view that we see in Washington is not reflective of Republican interests at large?

PAUL KRUGMAN: That's right, the committed Republican base is very right wing, and the committed Republican base and the Tea Party are basically the same thing. But if you take the broader group of self-identified Republicans, they have a lot of views that are considered left of centre in Washington. Of course if you look to the general public, they are against cutting social security, they are for higher taxes on the rich. The political process is not serving well as a reflection of what the public actually wants.

BRIAN MILNER: Does your optimism depend on them solving the impasse in Washington, and solving this dysfunction and the constant battering back and forth?

PAUL KRUGMAN: It's very hard to see how we can get an effective response to the economic crisis, or anything else, unless we break through that impasse. If President Obama proposed a measure honouring motherhood, the Republicans would vote against it, right? So yeah, it is terribly dysfunctional right now.

BRIAN MILNER: Do you see any of this changing, and what is your outlook for the 2012 election?

PAUL KRUGMAN: These are crazy times. As we are having this conversation, I've just learned that Newt Gingrich has surged into a lead in the Republican primary polls, so anything can happen. I think there is a range of possible outcomes. I'm afraid the most likely thing is probably a hamstrung government, it is President Obama re-elected narrowly, with a hostile Congress, and nothing gets done. Or President Romney, who is probably secretly reasonably sane, but with a crazy Congress, hamstrung, and nothing gets done. There is a possibility, it is within the range of things that could happen, that not only is Obama re-elected, but Nancy Pelosi returns as Speaker of the House. That might be an interesting change to the political environment. Even though the Democrats would not have 60 percent of the seats in the Senate, the shock of that might actually be enough to change things. But I am grasping at straws.

BRIAN MILNER: Maybe we should follow the Western European models, they stick economists in the top government jobs.

PAUL KRUGMAN: I actually think that's unfortunate. I've got no complaints about Mary Amiti or Lucas Papademos, but what on earth makes people think that they will have the political connections to accomplish what their predecessors could not? That seems unlikely, and it's not exactly as if economists have distinguished themselves in this crisis. I'd like to think I've done okay, but not everybody thinks so. In Europe's case they are imposing technocrats after three years in which the technocrats in Europe have been wrong about everything, so there is something kind of off about what's going on there.

BRIAN MILNER: I wanted to ask you about Occupy Wall Street, and how seriously we should take it as a movement of social and political change. Or do think it is temporary?

PAUL KRUGMAN: I don't know what will happen with the protests. It's obviously not a movement, it's not a Leninist movement with cohesive leadership and a clear-cut goal, but it gave voice to something that was not being said. There's a lot of dismay among the American public about what's happening, and not dismay of the type that Rush Limbaugh is trying to channel, but a "Hey, why are these people doing so well when they actually brought on the crisis, and why aren't we doing anything about jobs?" These sentiments were going unheard until a fairly rag-tag group of protestors started camping in various parks. We are not going to have mass mobilization of Occupy Wall Street protestors, but I think that the upsurge of people in the public saying "Hey, this is wrong, this is not what we should be doing" is going to continue. Maybe they will continue the protests, maybe not, but, in a way, the movement has already achieved a lot.

BRIAN MILNER: Because it is tapped into this mainstream feeling that is much more tapped in than say the Tea Party ever could, do you see it evolving into a third political party down the road?

PAUL KRUGMAN: I doubt it. Let's put it this way: there are plenty of Democrats who embody a lot of what these people are saying. It's not as if there is nobody in politics representing this point of view. You can say a lot of Democrats don't, but many do. If Occupy Wall Street was looking for a political candidate who would embody a lot of what they say they support, then Elizabeth Warren is running for Senate in Massachusetts. If my hopes come true, what will happen instead is not that Occupy Wall Street will become the third force, but rather that a major political party, and in practice the Democrats, makes itself over to be more appreciative of the issues that these people are raising.

BRIAN MILNER: Do you get a sense that that is happening?

PAUL KRUGMAN: It's hard to be sure. There has been a noticeable stiffening of spines among progressive Democrats in the last few months. If you look from members of Congress, through the Senate, and including the president, they have visibly, audibly started standing up more for the principles that they were elected to serve than they were before, so something is happening.

BRIAN MILNER: And you don't see that dissipating as soon as the election is over?

PAUL KRUGMAN: I hope not. I'd like to think that a lot of people have learned a lesson. In 2009, there was a strong tendency among people to say, "Okay, now I'm going to turn to the people who know how things work, like those guys on Wall Street." I don't think they are going to make that mistake again.

BRIAN MILNER: I have one parochial Canadian question that involves the Keystone pipeline project, which has been shoved off until after the election. I don't hear Americans say that they are willing to pay $4 or $4.50 a gallon for gasoline, but they do say "don't build this pipeline in our neighbourhood," even though they've got thousands of miles of pipeline crossing the state of Nebraska. They've stopped nuclear facilities, they've stopped alternatives to fossil fuel.

PAUL KRUGMAN: I think that's being a little unfair. Yeah, there were some progressives behaving badly on wind farms, but a lot of that's been pushed back now and some of those projects are proceeding. We've got these blue panels up on telephone polls in New Jersey, and I am pretty annoyed with my neighbours, who are liberals, when they start complaining about the blue panels. I'm actually still doing some homework on Keystone, but my understanding is that this is a seriously dubious project, and that the objections are not just numinous. There are real issues about environmental impact, including climate change impact, so Obama did the right thing by delaying it. He was certainly not in a position to cancel it, but it would have been premature to approve it based on what was clearly a flawed process.

BRIAN MILNER: Okay, well thanks so much.

PAUL KRUGMAN: Thank you.

LAWRENCE SUMMERS IN CONVERSATION
WITH BRIAN MILNER

BRIAN MILNER: I think we should start with the purpose of your visit, which is the Munk debate tonight, and the question that you are dealing with is, Is the North America heading into a Japan-style stagnation, with a weak economy and high unemployment? I wonder if I can get your thoughts on that statement and why you disagree.

LAWRENCE SUMMERS: The United States does have severe aggregate demand problems; there's a very strong case for a whole set of measures to stimulate aggregate demand and if those measures are not pursued there will be substantial costs for the American economy. On the other hand, our situation differs fundamentally from Japan's. If stock prices in the United States fell as much as they did in Japan, the Dow would be at 3,000. If the lost output relative to potential was as large as it was in Japan a decade in, we'd be 25 to 30 percent short of our potential to produce. The United States has an important macro-economic problem, but it remains the source of innovation, and the most crucial information technology sector; it remains possessed of a capacity for entrepreneurship. We are the only country in the world where you can raise your first hundred million dollars before you buy your first suit. And the United States possesses a resilience that few other countries possess. This is not the first time we've seen pessimism about the United States and concern about decline. John F. Kennedy believed that Russia would surpass the United States. In the early 1990s it was a common joke that the Cold War was over, and Japan and Germany had won. The United States has its problems, but they are the problems of industrial democracy — they are problems less profound, less structural and more resolvable than those in Europe or Japan. Japan's problems during the 1990s, when it was the weak outlier in the global economy, are something very different.

BRIAN MILNER: And I know you've professed confidence that U.S. institutions can respond to this, but there is a concern that Washington has become so dysfunctional that they are not making the right policy decisions and that that's going to cause problems.

LAWRENCE SUMMERS: Washington has its problems. There is risk of gridlock. On the other hand, in the two years — 2009 and 2010 — Washington engaged in more consequential actions passing through the Congress than at any time in the last forty years. If you add together

the Recovery Act, the financial regulation reform bill
[Dodd–Frank Wall Street Reform and Consumer
Protection Act], and the move to universal health care,
it was actually a more malleable and flexible system than
it has been in a very long time. I believe it is precisely
the capacity of Americans to reject complacency, to
arouse concern, which leads to the greater resilience of
the American system. Yes, if you look at the ten-year
deficit forecast we've got terrible issues. But we have ten-
year deficit forecasts; they don't have those in Europe
or in Japan, and that's the reason we are more likely to
address our problems. I don't minimize the difficulties in
the United States. But again, I come back to these problems: too much debit, too little demand, people thinking
things are going in the wrong direction, crises of legiti-
macy and elites, fears about the damage that can come
from the financial sector — these are global problems. I
would argue that they are less serious global problems
in the United States than they are in Europe or in Japan.
In contrast, the Japanese situation you've just sited was
a situation of near total Japanese failure in a phase when
the global economy was actually working quite well,
when jobs were being created, when progress was being
made on a substantial scale in Europe and in the United
States, and that makes the Japanese situation a far more
troubling one than the American situation.

BRIAN MILNER: You have said that if policy-makers don't
do something different, and they stay on the track they
are currently on, that unemployment is going to be 8.5

percent at the end of 2012. That high unemployment rate is going to be a factor in the election. I'm wondering if you can comment both on your view of the presidential election, but also on this issue of what needs to be done to fix that broader problem.

LAWRENCE SUMMERS: I'm honoured to have worked for President Obama. I believe he is an extraordinary leader. I believe he should be re-elected. I expect that he will be re-elected. But beyond that I'm not going to get into politics. We need to make sure there is adequate demand in this economy. That means not withdrawing the contribution to demand provided by the Recovery Act when the economy is still fragile. That means making sure that America maximizes its opportunity to sell into a global economy, and particularly into the emerging markets that are growing rapidly. That means working to assure that business confidence is maximized. All of these are important priorities if we are going to take advantage of this moment.

BRIAN MILNER: Then I guess we should deal with the issue of fiscal severance. It sounds like you think there should be more, not less, and that they shouldn't try to phase out what they are doing now.

LAWRENCE SUMMERS: That's correct. At a time when private savings have grown and private investment has collapsed, it is natural to assume that government has to take up the slack. The observation that the private sector has boomed and that private investment has collapsed, answers the question of how the deficit will be financed — it will be financed out of all the saving that doesn't have a counterpart demand for investment. By acting as a balance, against the sharp changes that have taken place in the private sector, government can make an important contribution to stabilizing the economy.

BRIAN MILNER: I can't let you go without asking for a comment on what's happening in the eurozone and what your prognosis is.

LAWRENCE SUMMERS: It's very problematic. At every stage in a financial crisis there is the prospect that a focus on fundamentals will give way to panic, and investors will stop looking at underlying reality and start looking at other investors. I fear we've gotten very close to that line, or perhaps we went over that line last week.

BRIAN MILNER: Do you see the Euro surviving this crisis?

LAWRENCE SUMMERS: I think a great deal will depend upon the steps that are taken going forward.

BRIAN MILNER: I also want to ask you about Occupy Wall Street, are we looking at something significant or just a blip on the radar?

LAWRENCE SUMMERS: There is widespread concern and there certainly should be. We've had a financial accident roughly every three years for the last twenty-five.

If you think about the '87 stock market crash, the S&L debacle, the Mexican financial crisis, the Asian financial crisis, Russia/LTCM, the bursting of the Nasdaq bubble, most consequently the tragedy of the last five years. So, anxiety, anger, and demand for change with respect to the financial sector, is very much warranted. It is a very widely shared value. The question is really figuring out what's best to do and what can be done to preserve all the benefits of finance support for entrepreneurship, getting resources to best uses, without the risks of instability that we've seen — that's really the hugely important question for the years ahead.

BRIAN MILNER: Do you see it coalescing into a new political movement or a new political party, or will it be absorbed by the Democrats? How do you see that playing out?

LAWRENCE SUMMERS: If you look at history there are protest movements, and the most common thing is that when there are large protest movements, their message of concern is absorbed by continuing institutions and continuing political parties. So they do have an important impact. But, I would be surprised if there was a major political party based on the ideas of Occupy Wall Street. At this point, the ideas seem too inchoate to really provide a basis for an alternative approach to governing.

BRIAN MILNER: Thank you very much, Dr. Summers.

LAWRENCE SUMMERS: Thank you.

ACKNOWLEDGEMENTS

The Munk Debates are the product of the public-spirit-edness of a remarkable group of civic-minded organizations and individuals. First and foremost, these debates would not be possible without the vision and leadership of the Aurea Foundation. Founded in 2006 by Peter and Melanie Munk, the Aurea Foundation supports Canadian individuals and institutions involved in the study and development of public policy. The debates are the foundation's signature initiative, a model for the kind of substantive public policy conversation Canadians can foster globally. Since their creation in 2008, the foundation has underwritten the entire cost of each semi-annual debate. The debates have also benefited from the input and advice of members of the board of foundation, including Mark Cameron, Andrew Coyne, Devon Cross, Allan Gotlieb, George Jonas, Margaret MacMillan, Anthony Munk, and Janice Stein.

Since their inception the Munk Debates have sought to take the discussions that happen at each event to national and international audiences. Here the debates have benefited immeasurably from a partnership with Canada's national newspaper, the *Globe and Mail*, and the counsel of its editor-in-chief John Stackhouse.

With the publication of this superb book, House of Anansi Press is helping the debates reach new audiences in Canada and internationally. The debates' organizers would like to thank Anansi chair, Scott Griffin, and president and publisher, Sarah MacLachlan, for their enthusiasm for this book project and insights into how to translate the spoken debate into a powerful written intellectual exchange.

ABOUT THE DEBATERS

IAN BREMMER is the founder and president of Eurasia Group, a leading global political risk analysis and consulting firm. He is the author of several books, including the national bestseller, *The End of the Free Market*, and *The J Curve: A New Way to Understand Why Nations Rise and Fall*, which was selected by *The Economist* as one of the best books of 2006. Bremmer is a contributor for the *Wall Street Journal* and *Foreign Policy*, and he has published articles in the *Washington Post*, the *New York Times*, *Newsweek*, *Harvard Business Review*, and *Foreign Affairs*. He is a panelist for CNN International's *Connect the World*. Bremmer lives in New York and Washington, DC.

PAUL KRUGMAN is a columnist for the *New York Times*. He won the Nobel Prize in Economics for his groundbreaking work on international trade and economic geography. In addition to the Nobel Prize, Krugman's work in economics has earned him several prestigious awards, including the John Bates Clark Medal for his work on international trade. He has published several books, including the recent bestseller, *The Return of Depression Economics.* A previous book, *The Great Unraveling,* was a *New York Times* bestseller. Professor Krugman teaches economics and international affairs at Princeton University.

DAVID ROSENBERG is the Chief Economist and Strategist at Gluskin Sheff + Associates Inc., and the former Chief North American Economist at Bank of America Merrill Lynch. His economic analysis is frequently featured in *Barron's,* the *Globe and Mail,* the *Wall Street Journal,* and on CNBC. Rosenberg has been ranked first by economists in the Brendan Wood International Survey for Canada for the past seven years, and has been on the U.S. Institutional Investor American All-Star Team for the last four years. He ranked second overall in the 2008 Institutional Investors Survey for the United States. He lives in Toronto.

LAWRENCE SUMMERS has served as chief economist of the World Bank, U.S. secretary of the Treasury, president of Harvard, and most recently as President Obama's director of the White House National Economic Council. He served as a key policy-maker in the Treasury Department throughout the administration of President Bill Clinton, in the role of secretary of the Treasury from 1999 to

2001. He is one of the youngest tenured professors in the modern history of Harvard University, and he is the only social scientist to receive the National Science Foundation's $500,000 Alan T. Waterman Award for Scientific Achievement. He is also the recipient of the John Bates Clark Medal for his work in several fields of economics.

ABOUT THE EDITORS

RUDYARD GRIFFITHS is a co-host of the CTV News Channel current events show *National Affairs*. He is the co-director of the Munk Debates and the Salon Speakers Series. He is a co-founder of the Historica-Dominion Institute, Canada's largest history and civics NGO. In 2006, he was named one of Canada's "Top 40 under 40" by the *Globe and Mail*. He is the editor of twelve books on history, politics, and international affairs, and the author of *Who We Are: A Citizen's Manifesto*, which was a *Globe and Mail* Best Book of 2009 and a finalist for the Shaughnessy Cohen Prize for Political Writing. He lives in Toronto.

PATRICK LUCIANI is the co-director of the Munk Debates and the Salon Speakers Series. He was a former executive director of the Donner Canadian Foundation, and he has authored two books on economic issues. He is also the co-author of *XXL: Obesity and the Limits of Shame* with Neil Seeman. He lives in Toronto.

ABOUT THE MUNK DEBATES

The Munk Debates are Canada's premier public policy event. Held semi-annually, the debates provide leading thinkers with a global forum to discuss the major public policy issues facing the world and Canada. Each event takes place in Toronto in front of a live audience, and the proceedings are covered by domestic and international media. Participants in recent Munk Debates include Robert Bell, Tony Blair, John Bolton, Ian Bremmer, Paul Collier, Howard Dean, Hernando de Soto, Gareth Evans, Mia Farrow, Niall Ferguson, William Frist, David Gratzer, Rick Hillier, Christopher Hitchens, Richard Holbrooke, Henry Kissinger, Charles Krauthammer, Paul Krugman, Lord Nigel Lawson, Stephen Lewis, David Li, Bjørn Lomborg, Elizabeth May, George Monbiot, Dambisa Moyo, Samantha Power, David Rosenberg, Lawrence Summers, and Fareed Zakaria. The Munk Debates are a project of the Aurea

Foundation, a charitable organization established in 2006 by philanthropists Peter and Melanie Munk to promote public policy research and discussion. For more information visit www.munkdebates.com.

PERMISSIONS

Permission is gratefully acknowledged to reprint excerpts from the following:

(p. 59–68) "Paul Krugman in Conversation," by Brian Milner. Copyright 2011, *Globe and Mail*. Transcribed by Erin Kelly. Reprinted with permission.

(p. 69–74) "Lawrence Summers in Conversation," by Brian Milner. Copyright 2011, *Globe and Mail*. Transcribed by Erin Kelly. Reprinted with permission.

Graphs

(p. 28) "Japan GDP Growth" reprinted by permission of The Munk Debates. (Data from World Bank; http://data.worldbank.org/indicator/NY.GDP.MKTP.KD.ZG)

(p. 29) "Benchmark Interest Rate" reprinted by permission of The Munk Debates. (Data from TradingEconomics. com; Bank of Japan)

(p. 29) "Public Debt" reprinted by permission of The Munk Debates. (Data from OECD.STATExtracts "Total Central Govt Debt % of GDP," Stocks: Outstanding Amounts. http://stats.oecd.org/index. aspx?DataSetCode=GOV_DEBT)

Also available

Does the 21st Century Belong to China?
Edited by Rudyard Griffiths and Patrick Luciani

ISBN: 978-1-77089-062-6

Powered by the human capital of 1.3 billion citizens, the latest technological advances, and a comparatively efficient system of state-directed capitalism, China seems poised to become *the* global superpower this century. But the Middle Kingdom also faces a series of challenges. From energy scarcity to environmental degradation to political unrest and growing global security burdens, a host of factors could derail China's ascent.

On June 17, 2011, former U.S. Secretary of State Henry Kissinger and CNN's Fareed Zakaria squared off against leading historian Niall Ferguson and world-renowned Chinese economist David Daokui Li to debate China's emergence as a global force, the key geopolitical issue of our time.

 This edition of The Munk Debates — Canada's premier international debate series — features the first formal public debate Dr. Kissinger has participated in on China's future, and also includes candid interviews with Henry Kissinger and David Daokui Li.

Available in fine bookstores and at www.houseofanansi.com
Also available as an e-book

Also available

Hitchens vs. Blair
Edited by Rudyard Griffiths

ISBN: 978-1-77089-008-4

On November 26, 2010, intellectual juggernaut and staunch atheist Christopher Hitchens went head-to-head with former British prime minister Tony Blair, one of the Western world's most openly devout political leaders, on the highly charged topic of religion. Few world leaders have had a greater hand in shaping current events than Blair; few writers have been more outspoken and polarizing than Hitchens. In this edition of The Munk Debates — Canada's premier international debate series — Hitchens and Blair square off on the contentious questions that continue to dog the topic of religion in our globalized world: How does faith influence our actions? What is the role of people of faith in the public sphere? Is religious doctrine rigid, or should we allow for flexibility in our interpretations?

Sharp, provocative, and thoroughly engrossing, *Hitchens vs. Blair* is a rigorous and electrifying intellectual sparring match on the oldest question — Is religion a force for good in the world?

Available in fine bookstores and at www.houseofanansi.com
Also available as an e-book

Also available

The Munk Debates: Volume One
Edited by Rudyard Griffiths
Introduction by Peter Munk

ISBN 978-0-88784-248-1

Launched in 2008 by philanthropists Peter and Melanie Munk, the Munk Debates is Canada's premier international debate series, a highly anticipated cultural event that brings together the world's brightest minds.

This volume includes the first five debates in the series, and features twenty leading thinkers and doers arguing for or against provocative resolutions that address pressing public policy concerns, such as the future of global security, the implications of humanitarian intervention, the effectiveness of foreign aid, the threat of climate change, and the state of health care in Canada and the United States.

Intelligent, informative, and entertaining, *The Munk Debates* is a feast of ideas that captures the prevailing moods, clashing opinions, and most imperative issues of our time.

Available in fine bookstores and at www.houseofanansi.com
Also available as an e-book